EDWARDSVILLE PUBLIC LIBRAR

# SUPER STRUCTURES

## Paul Nash

*Some of the biggest structures on earth: office buildings, temples, aircraft hangars, stadiums, exhibition halls, telescopes, statues, factories, castles, antennas and towers, public buildings, apartments, chimneys — and a home!*

**GEC** GARRETT EDUCATIONAL CORPORATION

# CONTENTS and Picture Acknowledgments

| | | | |
|---|---|---|---|
| **The Pentagon** | 3 | **Ice sculpture** | 19 |
| U.S. Department of Defense | | Japan National Tourist Organization | |
| **Warsaw Radio Tower** | 4 | **Cooling tower** | 21 |
| Interpress Photoservice, Poland | | State Electricity Commission of Victoria | |
| **Filton Aircraft Hangar** | 5 | **Windsor Castle** | 23 |
| British Aerospace | | Nicholas Servian/Woodmansterne | |
| **Abu Simbel Temple** | 7 | **Sears Tower** | 24 |
| Egyptian State Tourist Office | | Courtesy of Sears, Roebuck & Co. | |
| **Louisiana Superdome** | 8 | **Sydney Opera House** | 25 |
| Facility Management of Louisiana, photo by Cliff Wallace | | Australian Information Service, London | |
| **Garden Festival Hall** | 10 | **CN Tower** | 26 |
| Arup Associates, London | | Canadian High Commission, London | |
| **Radio telescope** | 11 | **Moscow University** | 27 |
| University of Manchester Nuffield Radio Astronomy Laboratories, Jodrell Bank | | Novosti Press Agency | |
| | | **Barbican apartments** | 28 |
| | | John Laing Construction Ltd. | |
| **Soccer stadium** | 12 | **Chimney** | 30 |
| Brazilian Embassy, London | | INCO Ltd. | |
| **Giant bronze Buddha** | 15 | **London Telecom Tower** | 31 |
| Japan Information Centre, London | | Behram Kapadia | |
| **Boeing Aircraft Factory** | 17 | **Termite nest** | 32 |
| Boeing Commercial Airplane Company | | Australian Tourist Commission | |
| **Electricity transmission towers** | 18 | | |
| Central Electricity Generating Board | | | |

Text © copyright 1989 by Garrett Educational Corporation
First published in the United States in 1989 by Garrett Educational Corporation, 130 East 13th Street, Ada, OK 74820
First Published by Young Library Ltd., Brighton, England
© Copyright 1985 Young Library Ltd.

All rights reserved including the right of reproduction in whole or in part in any form without the prior written permission of the publisher. Published by Garrett Educational Corporation, 130 East 13th Street, P.O. Box 1588, Ada, Oklahoma 74820.

Manufactured in the United States of America

**Library of Congress Cataloging in Publication Data**

Nash, Paul, 1943-
  [Enormous edifices]
  Super structures / Paul Nash.
    p. cm.
  Rev. ed. of: Enormous edifices, © 1985.
  Summary: An introduction to some of the largest buildings on earth, including the Pentagon, Sears Tower, and the Moscow University.
  1. Tall buildings—Juvenile literature. [1. Tall buildings. 2. Buildings.] I. Title.
TH846.N34   1989
720′.483—dc20                                89-1200
     ISBN 0-944483-37-2                          CIP
                                                  AC

# THE PENTAGON

This is the world's largest office building, built to house the U.S. Defense Department's offices. It has a total floor area of 6,500,000 square feet (604,000 square meters, 150 acres). Instead of giving space to the 23,000 people who work there, you could spread out 83 football fields. The corridors in the building total 17.5 miles (28 kilometers) in length, but the compact shape of the five-sided building enables an office worker to walk from one office to any other in only seven minutes.

## WARSAW RADIO TOWER

This is the tallest structure in the world. The antenna, which transmits radio and TV broadcasts in Poland, towers 2,120 feet (646 meters) above ground level. Even if you stood three London Telecom Towers (see page 31) on top of each other, you would still not reach the top. It would take you ten minutes to walk along its length if it were lying on the ground. Weighing 541 tons (550,000 kilograms) the tower is supported by fifteen steel guy ropes. The transmitter on the tower is very powerful — 2,400 kilowatts, the power needed for 24,000 large electric light bulbs.

**Guy rope:** a wire or cable used to hold a structure which might otherwise shift its position.

## FILTON AIRCRAFT HANGAR

This is where the British Concorde airliner is built. It is the largest hangar building in Britain — 1,052 feet (321 meters) long and 420 feet (128 meters) wide. Three football fields would easily fit end-to-end inside the hangar with room to spare! Compare the size of the double-decker bus parked in front of the giant doors. They're the biggest doors in Britain, being 66 feet (20 meters) high and 1,045 feet (318 meters) long. The whole hangar has a total volume or capacity of 34,400,000 cubic feet (974,000 cubic meters), enough space to fit nearly a thousand houses in one big heap.

**hangar:** a garage for storing airplanes or a building for assembling them.

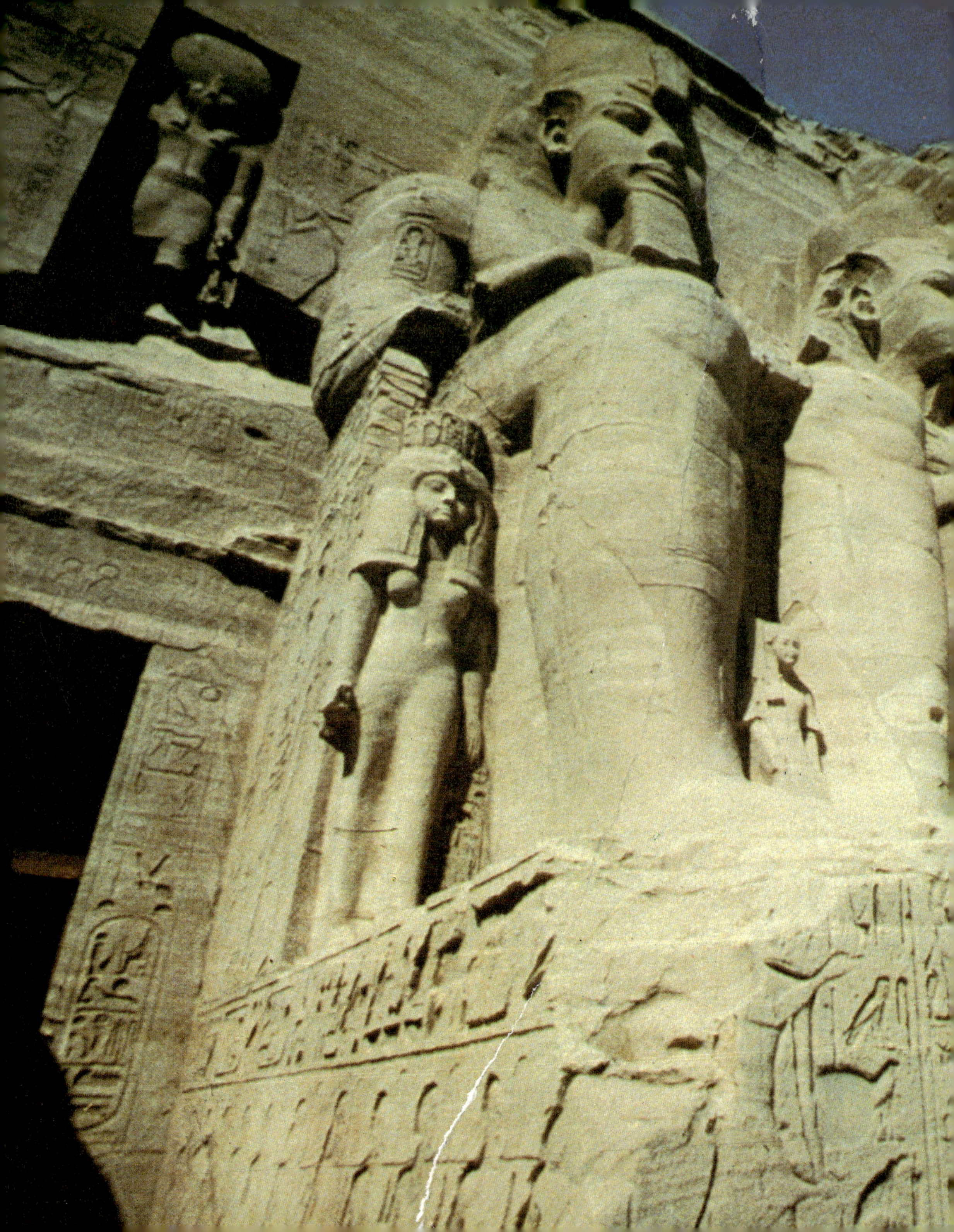

## ABU SIMBEL TEMPLE

These colossal stone figures were carved out of the rock on the bank of the Nile River, in Egypt, about 3,200 years ago. They represent the ruler Rameses II, and sit, two on each side, at the entrance of the Great Temple of Abu Simbel. The carved statues measure 67 feet (20 meters) from the headdress to the feet, and are the largest figures of Egyptian sculpture. When the level of the river was raised in 1966 for an irrigation/hydroelectric project, these giant figures were dismantled and rebuilt higher up on a man-made hill.

# LOUISIANA SUPERDOME

No, this is not an Unidentified Flying Object from outer space. It is the world's largest indoor stadium and the world's largest dome structure. It stands in the city of New Orleans in the United States. It can seat 76,800 spectators in comfort for a football game, or can allow over 100,000 people to enjoy a festival event. The dome that spans the arena is 680 feet (207 meters) in diameter, more than twice the length of a football field. The top of the dome is 273 feet (83 meters) above the ground, 47 times taller than a man. To make the Superdome, 17,900 tons of steel were used — enough for each spectator to have a quarter of a ton. The electrical wiring for the Superdome stretches for 400 miles (644 kilometers).

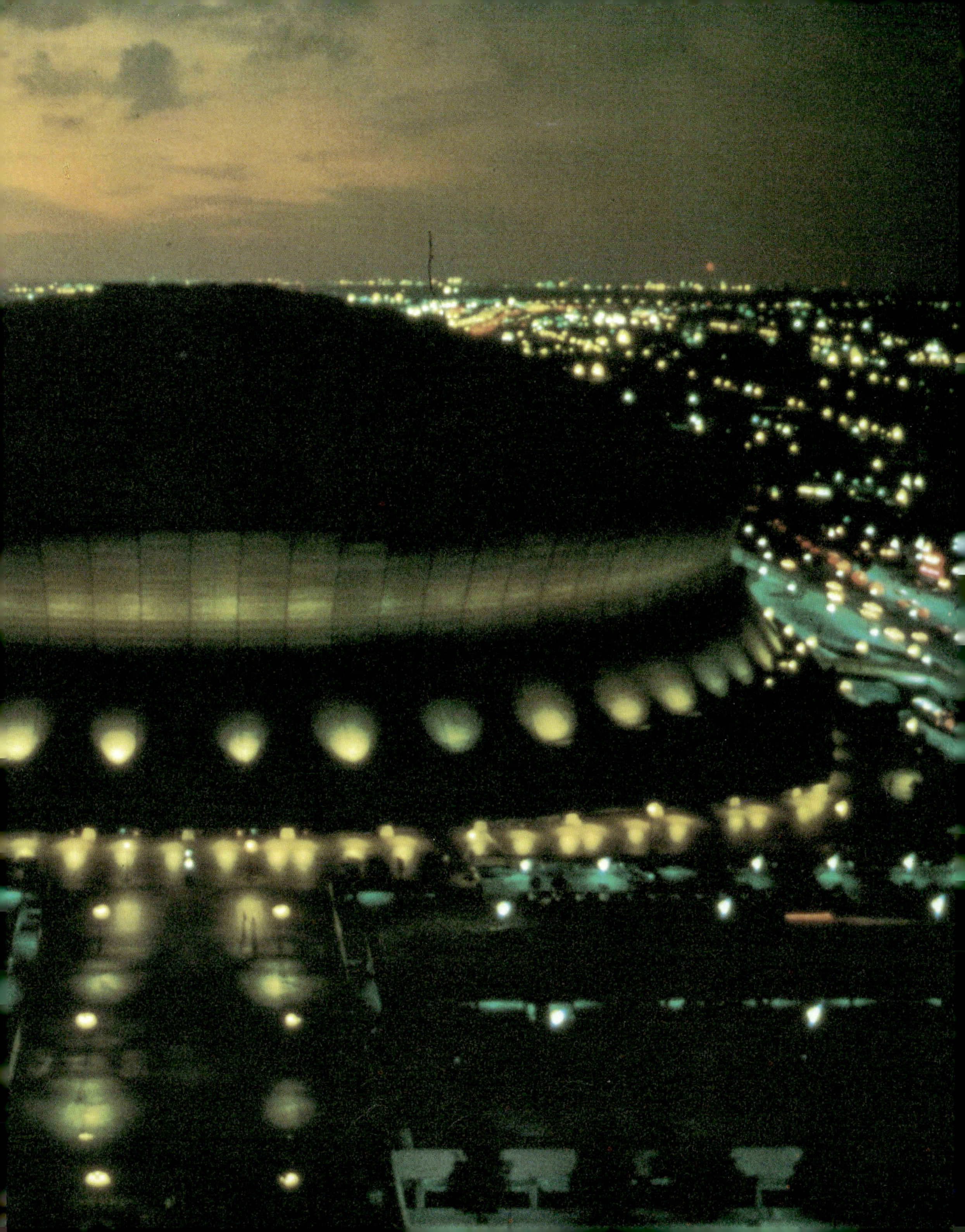

# GARDEN FESTIVAL HALL

This exhibition hall was built for the 1984 International Garden Festival in Liverpool, England. An area big enough for a football field is clad in special translucent plastic panels to let in light. The building is 453 feet (138 meters) long, and the roof curves from wall to wall with no supporting pillars to get in the way. The Festival Hall is built on ground that used to be an enormous sanitary landfill. The ground was landscaped into a beautiful garden ready for spring 1984.

**translucent:** a translucent material lets light shine through but is difficult or impossible to see through.

## RADIO TELESCOPE

Britain's largest single-dish radio telescope is at Jodrell Bank in Cheshire. The giant telescope dish is 250 feet (76 meters) in diameter. It would take 42 men touching fingertip-to-fingertip to reach across it. Motors of 150 horsepower turn the telescope dish slowly around. Turning it 180 degrees to face the opposite direction takes nearly 20 minutes. Rather slow, but not really surprising as it weighs 3,200 tons (3,250,000 kilograms).

## SOCCER STADIUM

The world's largest soccer stadium can hold 200,000 spectators. The Maracana Municipal Stadium in Rio de Janeiro, Brazil, is 1,045 feet (318 meters) at its widest diameter. It would take you 15 minutes to walk around the outside of the stadium, for it is nearly six-tenths of a mile (a kilometer). To allow nighttime soccer to be played, there are 220 floodlights, each 1,500 watts — equivalent to having all the lights on in 660 four-bedroom houses.

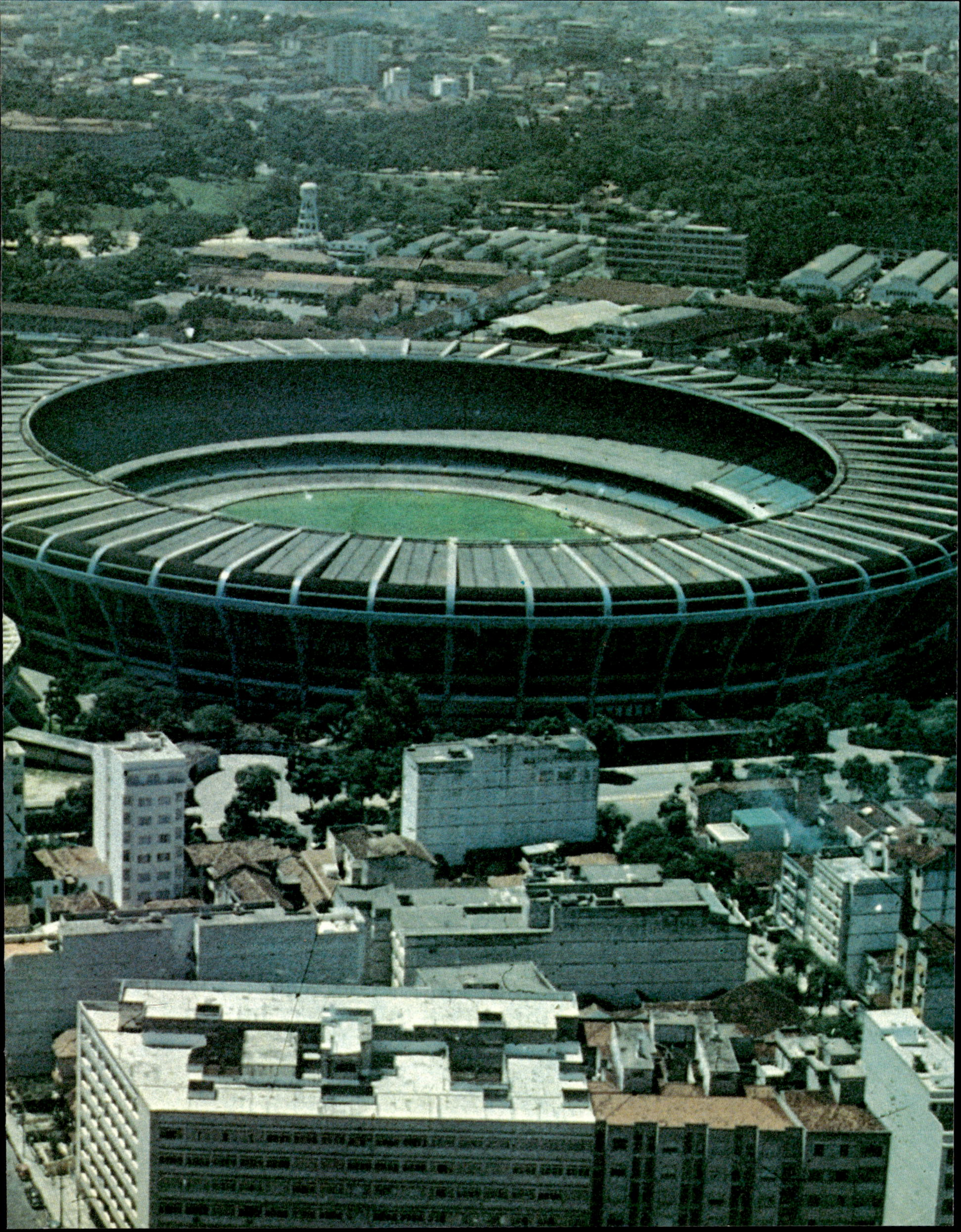

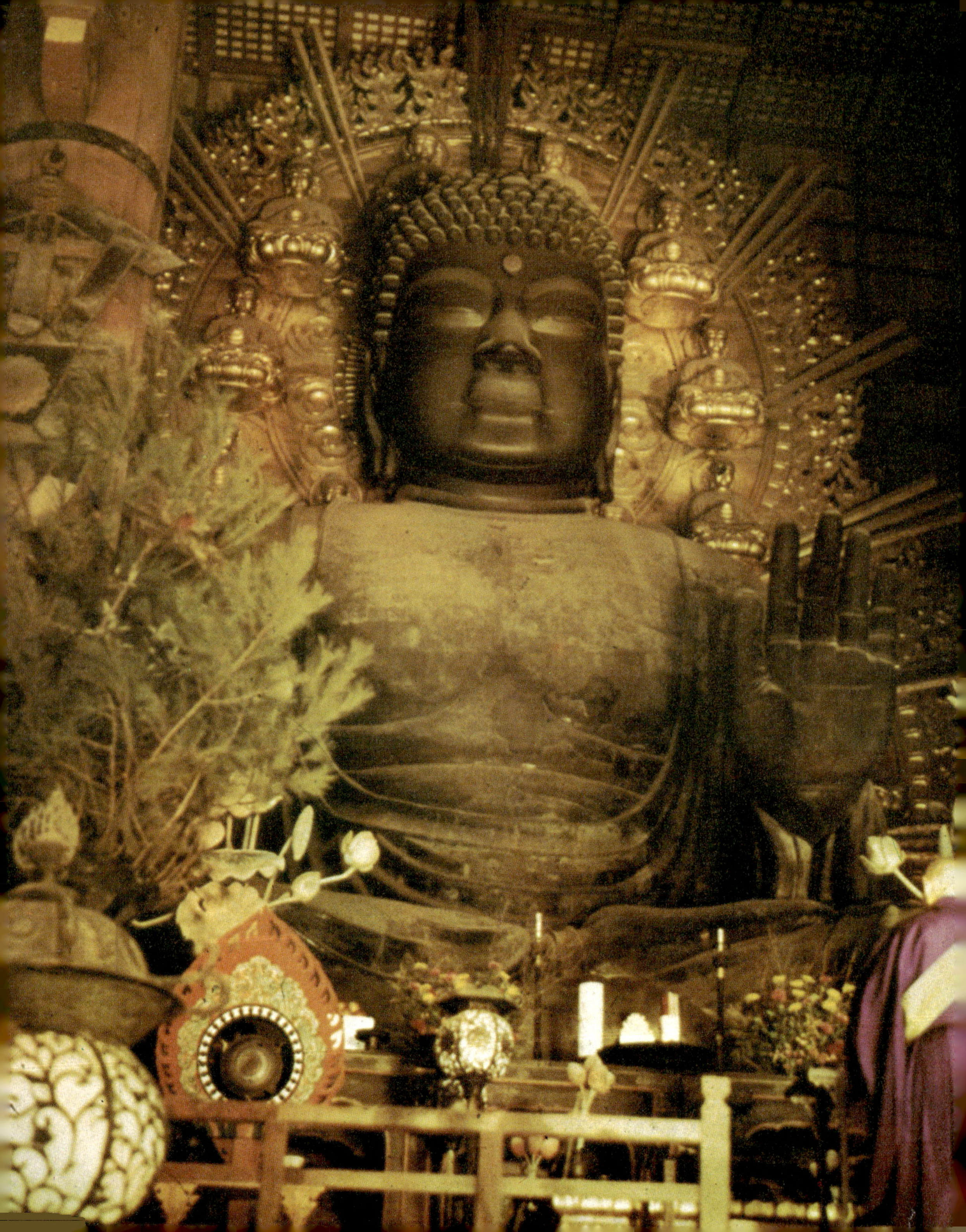

## GIANT BRONZE BUDDHA

The world's largest bronze statue of the Buddha is over 1,200 years old. Housed in a specially built temple in Japan, the Great Buddha of Nara is 53 feet (16 meters) high — nine times higher than a person. The statue was built by 8,000 people working for over ten years. The weight of the statue is not known accurately, and can only be estimated. It is probably 394 tons (400,000 kilograms), which is heavier than a jumbo jet airliner.

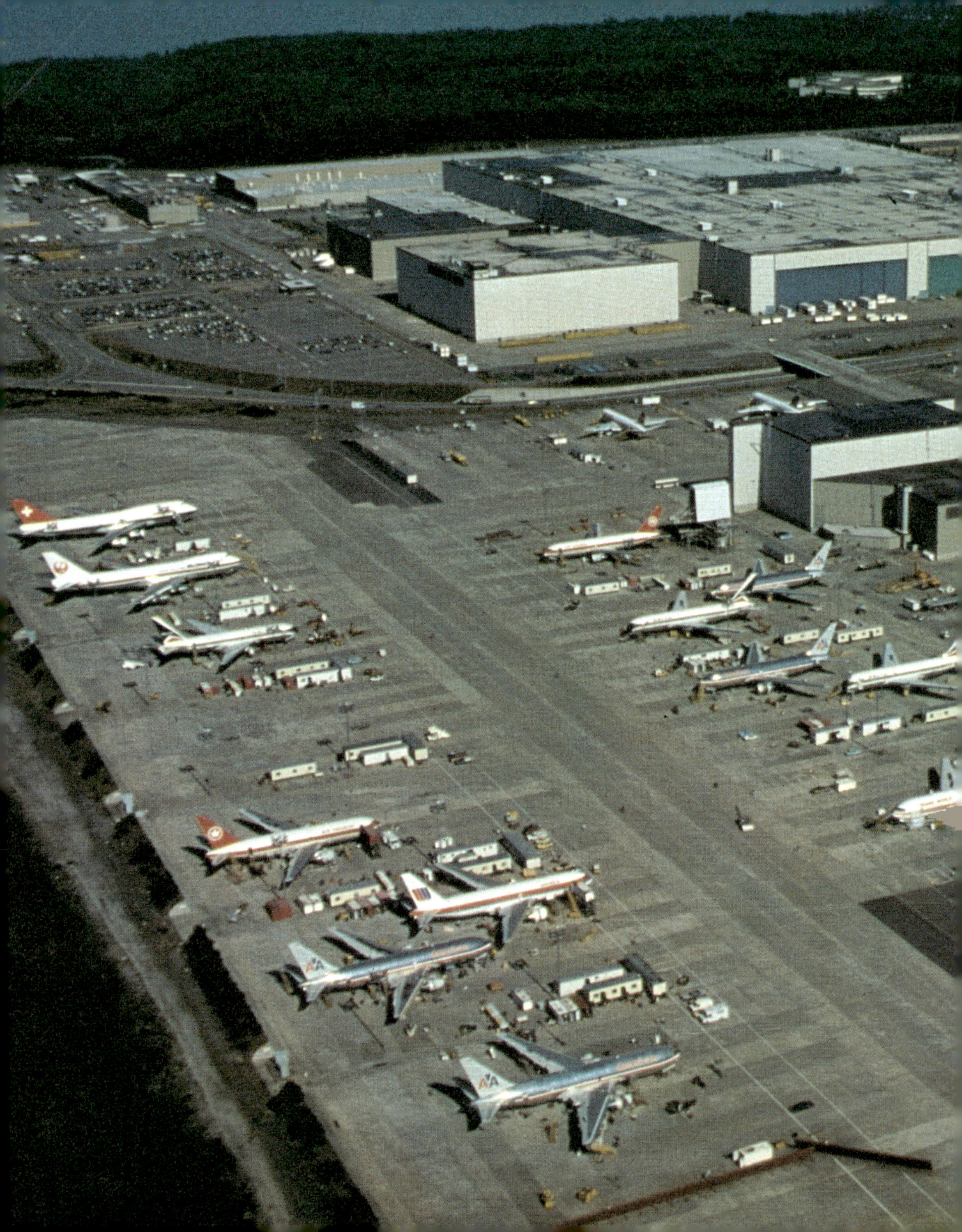

## BOEING AIRCRAFT FACTORY

This aircraft assembly building (seen in the background of the picture) is the world's most voluminous building. The largest passenger jet aircraft in the world — the Boeing 747 Superjet — is built here. Containing 290 million cubic feet (8,200,000 cubic meters) of space, the building is large enough to store over 8,000 houses. If all the water from Niagara Falls were let into the building, it would take nearly four hours to fill. Covering 62 acres (250,000 square meters) the entire plant is 2,068 feet (630 meters) long and 1,614 feet (492 meters) wide. That's over six times longer and nearly seven times wider than a football field.

## ELECTRICITY TRANSMISSION TOWERS

These electricity transmission lines across the Thames River hang from the tallest electricity transmission towers in Britain — 630 feet (192 meters) high. The electric cable carries electricity at 275,000 and 400,000 volts — that's 1,100 and 1,700 times greater than normal voltages. The steel electric cable is 4,500 feet (1,370 meters) long tower-to-tower — enough to wrap twice around the Superdome on page 8. It sags under its own weight, drooping to a minimum height of 250 feet (76 meters) above the river.

**ICE SCULPTURE**

This giant ice sculpture was made in Japan during the Yuki Matsuri — Snow Festival — which is held every year in Sapporo. Nearly 980 tons (1,000,000 kilograms) — over 300 truckloads — of snow were used to model this figure. It took 40 people working hard to mold and carve the ice statues, some 33 feet (10 meters) high.

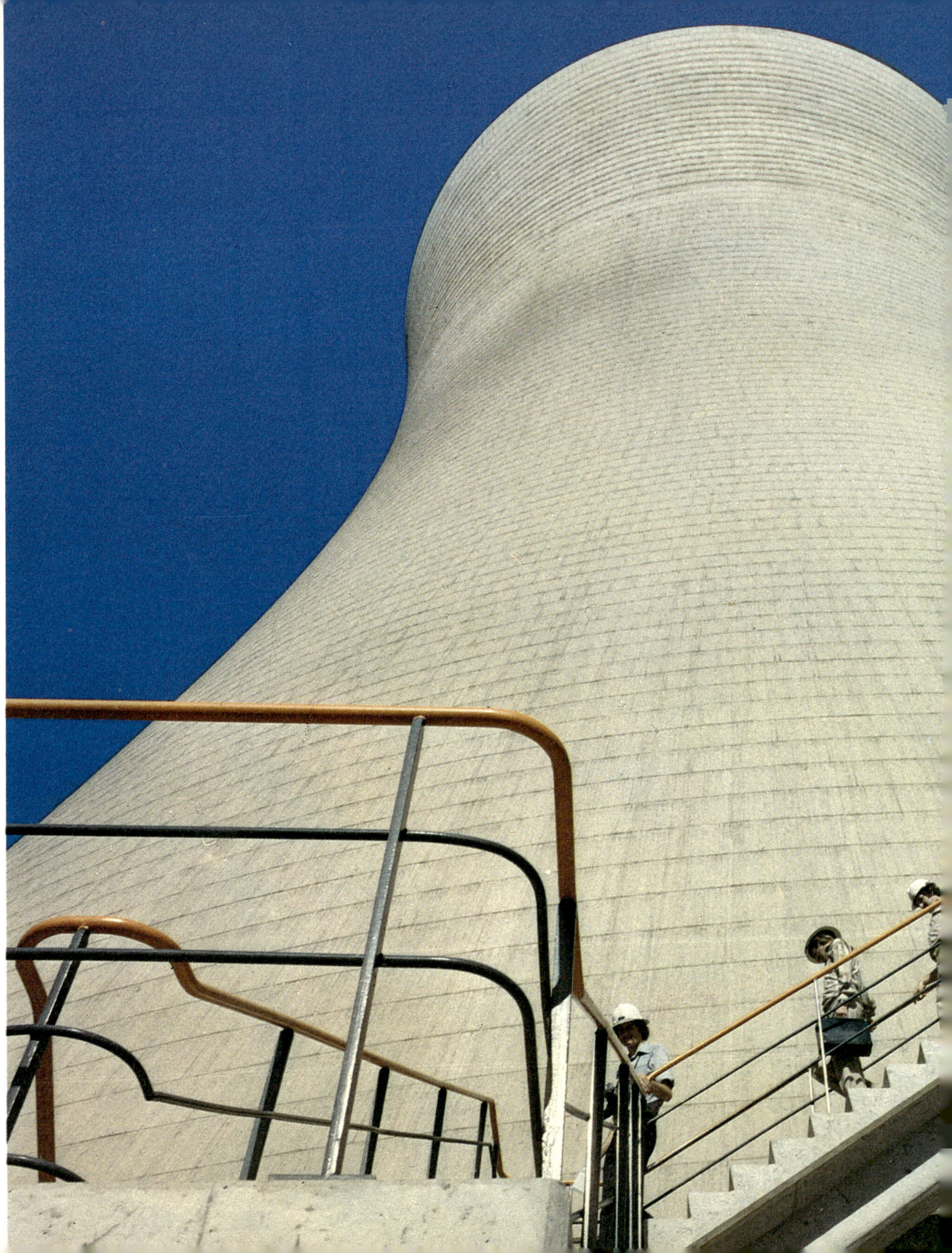

## COOLING TOWER

This giant cooling tower is in Australia. Sixty-five times as tall as a man, the tower is 375 feet (114 meters) high. It curves gently inwards from a 295-foot (90-meter) base, then broadens again to 166 feet (50 meters) at the top. The curve allows air to blow up the tower, cooling water which is sprayed down inside. The tower took 145,000 cubic feet (4,100 cubic meters) of concrete to make — enough to fill nearly a million large buckets.

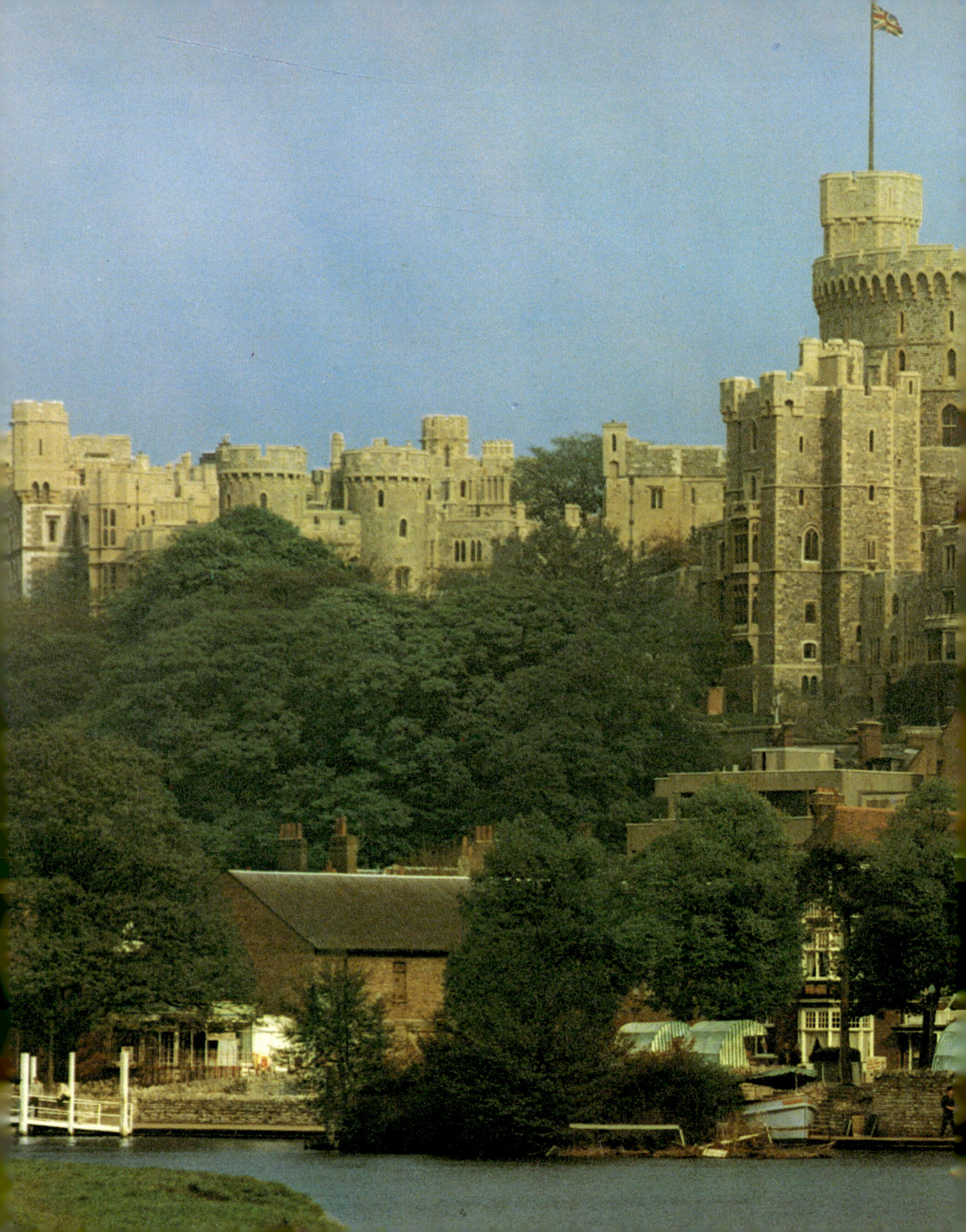

## WINDSOR CASTLE

This is the largest inhabited castle in the world. Windsor Castle, in Berkshire, England, covers 13 acres. First built 900 years ago, it is an official residence for the Queen. The central tower is 80 feet (24 meters) high, fourteen times taller than a man, with walls over 80 inches (2 meters) thick. The outer walls surrounding all the castle buildings are 1,890 feet (576 meters) long by 540 feet (164 meters) wide at their broadest point.

## SEARS TOWER

This is the world's tallest office building, rising 110 stories above Chicago, Illinois. The top of this office tower is 1,454 feet (443 meters) above ground level. Two TV antennas on top bring the height to 1,560 feet (475 meters). To equal that height you would need 270 people standing on top of each other. The floor area inside the building is a vast 101 acres (409,000 square meters) — nearly eight times more than Windsor Castle (page 23). With 16,000 windows, the window cleaners will never be out of work.

# SYDNEY OPERA HOUSE

This beautiful building which seats 7,000 people stands on the shore at Sydney Harbor in Australia. The white roof "shells" are made of concrete and covered with 1,000,000 tiles. To give the opera house plenty of light inside, there are over 2,000 panes of glass covering a total area of 65,000 square feet (6,100 square meters), about 1½ acres. The biggest sheet of glass weighs 1,100 pounds (500 kilograms), nearly 16 times heavier than the average reader of this book.

## CN TOWER

The tallest self-supporting tower in the world is in Toronto, Canada. Rising 1,820 feet (555 meters), it is almost three times taller than the London Telecom Tower (page 31). The rather small buildings beside it are skyscrapers! From the restaurant revolving 1,140 feet (347 meters) above the ground, diners can see the hills 75 miles (120 kilometers) away. Made of reinforced concrete, the tower weighs 128,000 tons (130,000,000 kilograms) — the same weight as 370 jumbo jets.

**reinforced concrete:** concrete containing steel bars, so that it withstands both crushing and stretching.

## MOSCOW UNIVERSITY

Standing on the Lenin Hills near Moscow is the largest university building in the world. Built about 30 years ago, it is 32 stories high and measures 787 feet (240 meters) to the top of its central tower. That is 135 times taller than a man, and more than twice the height of the giant cooling tower on page 21. Inside the building there are 40,000 rooms.

**stories**: the floors or levels of a building.

## BARBICAN APARTMENTS

In the heart of the City of London is the tallest apartment building in Britain. Called the Shakespeare Tower, in the Barbican, it rises 419 feet (128 meters) with 116 apartments on 44 stories. The surrounding buildings in the Barbican complex include a theater which houses the Royal Shakespeare Company, a concert hall for the London Symphony Orchestra, three motion-picture theaters, and an art gallery. One of the movie theaters is 70 feet (21 meters) below street level, which puts it 17 feet (5 meters) below sea level.

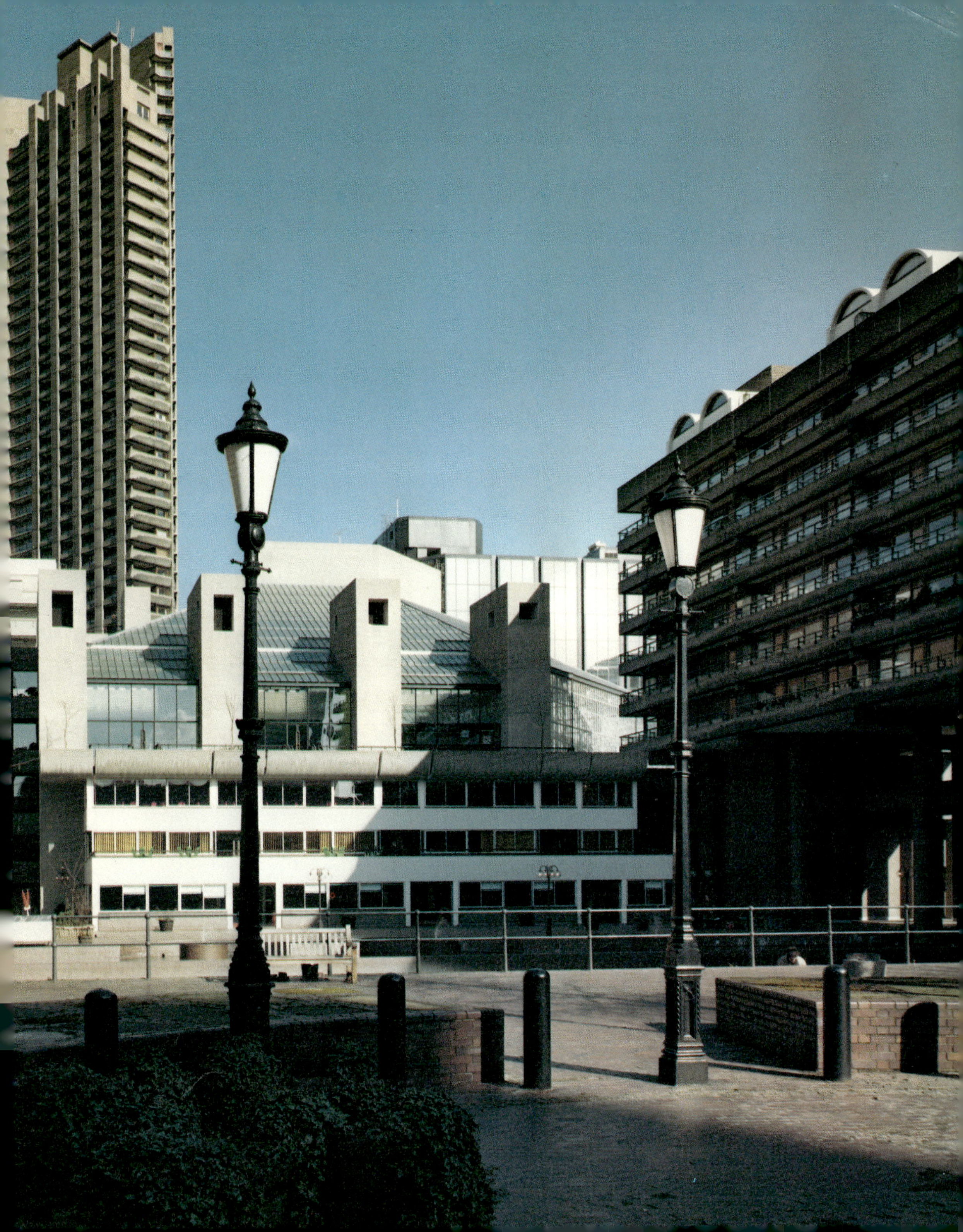

## CHIMNEY

This is the world's tallest chimney. It towers 1,244 feet (380 meters) above the ground in Ontario, Canada. The top is twice the height of the London Telecom Tower opposite. At the bottom the giant chimney is 116 feet (35 meters) wide, with 42-inch (107-centimeter) thick walls. At the very top it has narrowed to 56 feet (17 meters) wide with 11-inch (27-centimeter) walls. Its total weight is a massive 38,400 tons (39,000,000 kilograms) — the same as 6,100 elephants. There is enough concrete in this chimney to fill 194,000 wheelbarrows.

# LONDON TELECOM TOWER

Built 20 years ago, the London Telecom Tower is still the tallest building in London, at 620 feet (189 meters). Mounted on the tower are antennas for TV broadcasting and for radio transmission of telephone calls. Near the top of the tower is a revolving restaurant which gives you a view of London while you eat your meal. (You can see the view for yourself if you look at the front cover of this book.) To reach the restaurant you go in one of Britain's fastest elevators, traveling at 1,000 feet (305 meters) per minute — that's three times the height of a man every second.

# TERMITE NEST

The tallest building we have seen so far in this book is 270 times the height of a man. Here is a structure in Australia towering 600 times the height of its builders. It was made by termites, antlike creatures no bigger than your thumb nail.